T0272214

BEACH HOUSES

BEACH HOUSES

Coastal Homes of the World

CONTENTS

INTRODUCTION   7

OCEAN DECK HOUSE   11

MALIBU BEACH HOUSE   27

CASA KALIKA   33

TULUM VILLA   41

THE WHITE HOUSE   51

CASA KIMBALL   57

FRANGIPANI   69

VILLA AZUL CELESTE   79

SEA RANCH   93

CASA ALTIPLANO   105

LA CASA   115

LAZY LIZARD   125

AVE HOUSE   131

OLEANDER   139

ST IVES   149

ELIA VILLA   157

DEZANOVE HOUSE   167

AZURIS   177

SEGEDIN HOUSE   191

ALINGHI BEACH HOUSE   201

LINK HOUSE   217

SEASCAPE   229

FRESHWATER HOUSE   247

AMANZI KAMALA   259

OUTDOOR BEACH STYLE   275

INTRODUCTION

INTRODUCTION

*"The ocean stirs the heart, inspires the imagination
and brings eternal joy to the soul."*
Robert Wyland, marine life artist

Earth is blessed with five great oceans – the Atlantic, Pacific, Indian, Antarctic and Arctic. Romantically and historically speaking, Earth is also often said to have 'seven seas'. No matter which number you attest to, planet Earth is seventy one per cent water. That's a vast expanse of coastline to aspire to living by.

We too, on average, are sixty percent water. We are nearly the same mass as water, enabling us to float. Water is very much a part of who we are and since time began, we've been captivated by the sea.

Our ancestors came from the sea – evolving to who we are today. We spend the first nine months of life in the liquid surrounds of our mother's uterus.

Many dream of living an idyllic existence by the sea. For more fortunate others it's a wonderful reality. In fact, approximately eighty percent of the earth's people live within 100 kilometers (sixty-two miles) of the coastline of an ocean or other bodies of water.

There's something about the sea that attracts and mesmerizes us. We're inspired by it, the sound of the ocean and the scent of it in the breeze.

From walking along the shoreline with waves gently lapping our toes to diving headfirst under a wave; fishing in it to surfing or sailing upon it; writing about it; painting or photographing it – the ocean connects with us.

We know intuitively that being by the sea makes us happier, healthier, less stressed and more peaceful. Studies have shown people living near the sea are happier than their land-locked counterparts.

Little wonder we dream of owning a coastal home to live out our days.

Be it a simple, relaxed beach life or a more glamorous and aspirational verve, the coastal home design aesthetic is perennial in its appeal.

Light, airy, calm and the embodiment of natural beauty – coastal home design goes beyond kitsch seashells and nautical themes.

Showcased in this book is a broad snapshot of seaside living at its very best – a collection of some of the world's most stunning waterfront properties, award-winning architecture, lavish interiors and spectacular views. A selection of innovative and striking coastal projects from around the globe – the variety reflects the countries diverse style, landscape and environment.

Whether it's the sound of the surf in your ears that you long for, views to die for or the feel of sand between your toes – you will be drawn to these coastal homes and the lifestyle they embody.

Take this collection of homes and be inspired to create your own 'coastal' abode, in your own personal style.

From the more traditional Hampton's style to the contem-porary; modern; minimalist; ecological; bohemian; rustic; cottage or bungalow; Mediterranean, Scandinavian or Asian – coastal homes are much more than whites, blues and neutrals. Enjoy.

OCEAN DECK HOUSE

OCEAN DECK HOUSE

Bridgehampton, New York

Ocean Deck House, an exceptional beachfront residence in Bridgehampton, New York, is pure architectural porn for those who love to entertain.

Designed by Stelle Lomont Rouhani Architects for an energetic family who love nothing more than to cook and entertain, the strategy was to capture the sense of indoor-outdoor living with large cantilevered decks, roof decks and an open plan layout.

With 1,367 square meters (14,714 square feet) of living space, the ability to accommodate gatherings on each level was a driving element of the design. Maintaining the integrity of the sand dune, the property was pulled back from it to create three distinct experiences on each level.

The main floor of the ocean front residence is accessed from an exterior cantilevered stair that leads to the central light filled atrium. This main level houses all the bedrooms and a centrally located family room.

As a measure to preserve the integrity of the sand dune, the house is pulled back from it to create three distinct experiences on each level. The home mixes the natural beauty of polished wood with the permanence of concrete, outdoor fireplace and pool.

Photos by Matthew Carbone

The house was designed as an 'upside down' house, gifting the most stunning views to the living, dining and kitchen areas on the top floor and allowing direct access to the main, rooftop deck which is a seriously beautiful spot to throw a party.

The ground entrance level, which is nestled behind the sand dunes, showcases a mixed wood and concrete paved patio with a pool, outdoor fireplace and covered table tennis area.

The main floor is accessed from an exterior cantilevered stair that leads to the central light-filled atrium.

This main level houses all the bedrooms, a centrally located family room and the main deck is home to an extensive herb and vegetable garden and outdoor cooking area.

Seamless indoor-outdoor living is captured by introducing large cantilevered decks and roof decks, designed for entertaining.

With endless ocean views, space and seating for a crowd, the top floor is the social hub of the home when it comes to partying under the stars and string lighting.

Contemporary beach luxury with exquisite use of white, greys and muted blues. Wood and concrete combine with soft furnishings for cosy ambience without distracting from the hero of the property – the view.

The central light-filled stair case and atrium is enclosed by a combination of glass and concrete walls. The white, blue and neutral aesthetic is contemporary Hamptons at its best.

Overlooking gardens created by landscape architect Edmund Hollander with the ocean on the horizon couldn't be more delightful.

MALIBU BEACH HOUSE

MALIBU BEACH HOUSE

Malibu

Architect Richard Meier was forced to rethink his signature architectural style of using white when the mogul owner of this Malibu beach home commissioned him to design his new abode.

The house, clad entirely in teak shutters that can be opened or shut like an accordion, extends inside and out as floor to ceiling finishes.

Meier says of his design, "The opportunity to design an oceanfront residence is a privilege that cannot be overstated. The site for this house and guesthouse is exceptional in its size and the amount of ocean frontage it enjoys compared to other properties on this south-facing Malibu beach."

Photos by Simon Watson

CASA KALIKA

CASA KALIKA

Punta Mita, Mexico

With sensational crystal clear water views of the Pacific Ocean's Bay of Banderas, this is every golf fanatic's dream location – Casa Kalika is set on the ninth fairway of the Jack Nicklaus Golf Course within the Four Seasons Punta de Mita community.

Architect Guillermo Michel Renteria drew upon modern Balinese influences for the contemporary tropical palapa-style design, building the home with traditional, natural and organic materials, making the most of the indoor-outdoor flow.

Boasting five bedrooms and six bathrooms, the property is an impressive 930 square meters (10,000 square feet) of fluid spaces. With an infinity saltwater pool, wet bar and three jacuzzis to choose from, the perfect margarita sipping spot is never far.

The large open living and dining area covered with a palapa thatch roof with crystal blue water views of the Bay of Banderas is a favorite of the owner Fabienne Dufourg. "You are very in touch with nature and the amazing views change every hour," he says. Architect Guillermo Michel Renteria says "I wanted to create a sexy and airy home that integrates the beautiful Punta Mita environment with multiple elements including natural rocks, stone walls, exotic woods, fountains, landscape and interior patios. The elements of nature flow together within the open house where one room stretches into the next, leading to an infinity pool with an exotic cabana overlooking the bay."

Sue Chitpanish of Dao Home and owner Fabienne Dufourg used innovative design to create a relaxing 'zen' interior. Sue and Fabienne utilized organic custom furniture made of precious thick hardwoods from Bali, antique statues, local Mexican art and paintings, recycled glass vases and reclaimed wooden furniture to compliment the Philippe Stark contemporary furniture.

"Every piece of the décor was either custom made in Bali, Los Angeles or brought back from our trips," says Fabienne.

One of the luxurious four master suites, three with king size beds and the fourth with two beds. All complete with en suite bathrooms featuring sunk-in marble Jacuzzi bathtubs opening up to lush landscape gardens, inside and outside showers.

TULUM VILLA

TULUM VILLA/CASA XIXIM

Soliman Bay, Yucatan

Ecological luxury at its finest, Tulum Villa (also known as Casa Xixim) makes the most of its stunning natural surroundings. Perched on the beachfront of the turquoise blue waters near Tulum and backing onto the lush vegetation of the jungle, the property brings together modern architecture, traditional building practices and permaculture principles to blend in.

Situated on the Riviera Maya, Bahía de Soliman is a tranquil turquoise bay alive with a coral reef and wildlife.

The line between interior and exterior is a blurred one with screened wood louvers instead of glass windows to allow the fragrant sea breeze to waft throughout the home. In some spaces, windows and walls have been removed completely to allow the azure ocean views and gentle swaying palm trees to engulf the property.

The four-bedroom design includes huge living spaces, lower-level and rooftop terraces, an outdoor pool, native tropical garden and inviting hammocks sprinkled throughout.

Sustainability is key with the home running on solar power, featuring a green roof collecting rainwater as well as recycling and composting practices.

The native tropical garden supplies the owners with home-grown bananas, coconuts, vegetables and herbs.

THE WHITE HOUSE

THE WHITE HOUSE

Santa Teresa, Costa Rica

You'll feel the sand in your toes in this architectural piece of heaven on the beachfront of Playa Hermosa, just north of Santa Teresa in the Mal Pais area of Puntarenas, Costa Rica.

Designed by Los Angeles architect, Michael Poirier of Poirier Designs, the contemporary design influenced by the local 'Tico Style' of Costa Rica allows an indoor/outdoor holiday experience, no matter the weather, in this pristine location known for its large surf. Poirier drew inspiration from the tropical aesthetics of Miami, Thailand and Costa Rica for this holiday home built at the edge of the high tide line and next door to exclusive yoga resort, Pranamar.

The construction is a constant concrete framework with wood ceilings and floor to ceiling frameless glass allowing the lines of interior and exterior to blur.

The double-height spaces and large overhangs offer protection from the local climate conditions which vary from the extreme heat and sun in the dry season to the monsoonal rains in the wet season.

With the Pacific Ocean literally as your backyard, there are beach views from almost every room in this three-bedroom home.

The master bedroom, situated on the top floor, enjoys generous proportions with polished concrete floors, private bathroom, king-size bed and large covered balcony extending the room outdoors.

Downstairs, just beneath the master bedroom, is the poolside queen room with a view and easy access to the deck and stunning infinity pool whilst the back bedroom features two single beds – a peaceful retreat from the action.

The gourmet chef kitchen, also with incredible ocean view, allows for meal preparation with a side of sunset at the end of the day.

The living space is the real 'Pura Vida' – a term popular in Costa Rica, which translates to 'Pure Life' in English, but to Costa Rican people has a far more profound meaning – allowing for spirited or relaxed gatherings for family and friends.

Rattan outdoor furniture and wooden sunbeds allow for relaxing choices poolside.

CASA KIMBALL

CASA KIMBALL

Dominican Republic

Just east of Playa Grande in Cabrera, you'll find Casa Kimball, an exclusive eight-bedroom villa on the north coast of the island of the Dominican Republic.

The stunning Caribbean getaway was designed by New York architectural firm, Rangr Studio, for a New York client wanting a space large enough to accommodate his family and friends.

Situated on a cliff with a panoramic view of the Atlantic Ocean, the villa is approximately 1,850 square meters (20,000 square feet).

The jawdropping 45-meter (148 foot) infinity edge pool that appears to flow into the Atlantic Ocean is the focal point of the property.

One of the stunning bedrooms of the eight-bedroom villa can accommodate up to eighteen people.

The villa features two indoor and two outdoor lounges, a dining room with an impressive custom-made table for 20 that takes in a breathtaking view centered on the 45 meter (49 yard) infinity edge pool out to the ocean and outdoor bar area. A jacuzzi at the cliff's edge showcases the power of the ocean as waves crash on the rocks below.

The design is contemporary and constructed of reinforced concrete, clad with local coral stone, with buildings designed to optimize privacy, protecting views from neighboring properties.

The windows, constructed of dense Brazilian hardwood, swivel on wheel bearings, to allow interior spaces to merge with the exterior and cool ocean breezes to waft through the home.

The villa is nestled on three acres of oceanfront property surrounded by coco palms, almond trees, flowering vines and native trees.

A pathway along the cliff leads to a hidden terrace cut into the rocks with a fire pit as its centerpiece, an amazing location to contemplate life with a cocktail. The pathway continues to a private beach hidden away at the bottom of the cliff.

The dramatic infinity edge pool extends right to the sea cliff edge, taking in the expansive ocean views with a choice of sunbathing and seating options.

The infinity edge pool also features an oceanfront Jacuzzi for a dramatic clifftop experience. Its discreet location is not visible from any point on the property.

Even the bathtubs take advantage of the amazing view.

This luxury private estate is situated on three acres (1.2 hectares) of pristine property facing the Atlantic Ocean surrounded by almond trees, coco palms and many flowering vines and shrubs native to the Dominican Republic.

The contemporary design features floor to ceiling windows constructed of dense Brazilian hardwood that swivel on wheel bearings to allow interior spaces to merge with the exterior.

The villa features a dining room with an impressive custom-made table that seats 20.

Landscaped gardens add to the indoor/outdoor ambience of the villa.

Photos by Paul Warchol

FRANGIPANI

FRANGIPANI

Jumby Bay Island, West Indies

A long meandering driveway through a lush tropical landscape is your welcome to this stunning Caribbean-style estate.

The four-bedroom luxury villa sits on a secluded oceanfront property, positioned to take advantage of the cooling trade winds for natural ventilation. The rooms of the home are oriented to face the ocean and the breathtaking view. Rooms are configured around a grand outdoor living and dining pavilion with sweeping panoramic ocean views.

Perfect for entertaining, the home features a professional kitchen, dining table that accommodates 12 guests, barbecue area and family room with a built-in daybed to comfortably accommodate extra guests. The villa has four bedrooms, five bathrooms, a private beach, swim dock and a freshwater swimming pool with trellised seating area.

Frangipani sits at the end of a long meandering driveway, passing through a mature and lush tropical landscape.

Frangipani features its own private beach of blinding white sand and swim dock as well as a freshwater swimming pool with trellised seating area.

The house features bright colors, open-sided rooms and vaulted ceilings lend irresistible charm to the interiors of Frangipani. The kitchen, living and dining rooms feature casual arrangements of white-painted furniture with cheerful blue upholstery with accents of yellow. Most of the rooms in Frangipani face the stunning azure blue ocean, configured around the outdoor living and dining pavilion.

VILLA AZUL CELESTE

VILLA AZUL CELESTE

Puerto Vallarta, Mexico

Perched above the sea on the Bay of Banderas, is one of Puerto Vallarta's most sophisticated and exclusive hillside locations, Conchas Chinas. Here you'll find Villa Azul Celeste.

With stunning panoramic views of the Pacific Ocean from all levels of the three-bedroom, 3.5-bathroom abode, Villa Azul Celeste boasts relaxed luxury from the moment you step inside the courtyard entry of the villa which boasts 372 square meter (4,000 square feet) of interior space and an additional 186 square meter (2,000 square feet) of terraces, gardens and a dreamy, heated infinity pool.

Acclaimed local designer Peter Bowman created the vibrant interiors, which feature traditional Mexican furniture, artefacts, an extensive folk art collection, terracotta floors and antique hand-hewn beamed ceilings overhead.

Villa Azul Celeste is nestled into Conchas Chinas, Puerto Vallarta's most exclusive hillside neighbourhood.

With sapphire waters lapping your private beach and cove, the master bedroom suite on the second floor with king bed, fireplace and open shower for two is romance personified.

Two guest bedrooms are situated poolside. One features a king bed and large garden bath with a sculptured rock formation while the other also boasts a king bed and large private bath. Owner Sharon Tognietti explains how she found and fell in love with the home.

"In August 2010 my husband and I were on a short 4 day visit to Puerto Vallarta. A realtor friend of ours took us to look at homes just for fun. After viewing 11 homes in one afternoon we headed for our last showing," says Sharon. "Imagine our surprise when we first opened the door of Villa Azul Celeste. From the courtyard entry it seemed nice but once the doors opened we were in total shock."

"A perfectly framed picture of old world charm with the ocean as a backdrop. Terra cotta floors and rough-hewn beamed ceilings framed the picture. The home has a magical charm to it, all inspired by nature," she adds. "The house is a Vallarta Style house. Open to the elements. No doors or windows in the common areas. It just felt like home the minute we opened the door."

As if staged for Sharon's benefit, a pod of whales chose that moment to breach right before their eyes from the dining area.

"We were sold!" reveals Sharon. "The decor was dated so everything was replaced with the exception of the antique pieces. Mexican folk art was purchased including local Huichol Indian beaded pieces and Oaxacan textiles and black pottery. All the textiles are made with vegetable dyes and hand loomed," explains Sharon. "We wanted to showcase the arts and crafts of Mexico. Our collection is extensive and ongoing. The art is fun and colorful. No structural modifications were necessary as the home was perfectly planned. We wanted to keep the feel of Vallarta Style and not upset the balance nor modernize it."

Sharon's favorite room is the master suite. "It is the entire second floor. It has an outside terrace covered by a typical palapa style roof with ocean vistas to enjoy in complete privacy. There's seating for four, a stone fountain, a four-poster bed and Huichol Indian yard art pieces," she says. "The cupola shower is open to the elements with outstanding views.

Traditional Mexican furniture graces the terra cotta floors and antique hand-hewn beamed ceilings hang overhead over the master bedroom suite, featuring rustic four poster bed and private terrace.

SEA RANCH

SEA RANCH

Mornington Peninsula, Australia

Although not a registered architect, developer and builder, Daryl Turnbull, has designed and constructed enough high-end residences in the southern suburbs of Melbourne to know what he wanted for his design on the stunning coast of the Mornington Peninsula in Victoria.

Sea Ranch's design vision was to construct a visually stimulating monolithic structure with the use of Anthra black VM Zinc sheeting nestling into the coastal hillside on a stone base.

Although the use of the zinc was intentionally dominant, the selection of the flat lock panel system, which is quite textured and organic, adds interest and helps to soften the building. The use of natural materials and a natural color palette allow it to blend seamlessly into the bush surround.

The result set a new benchmark for architecture and luxury in Wye River. The sophisticated open plan design embraces the light and showcases every aspect of the almost unbelievable view. The breathtaking four-bedroom home offers views of the ocean, beach and windswept coastline.

Set a mere 50 meters (55 yards) above the crashing sea below, the sights and sounds of the ocean take care of any worries or stress levels before you nestle in beside a roaring fire in the living area.

Photos by John Wheatley

Sea Ranch offers a wondrous nature experience. All manner of Australian fauna have made themselves at home in the surrounding trees including koalas, king parrots, rosellas, cockatoos and kookaburras. Echidnas also make an appearance regularly, meandering through the garden.

It has a luxurious master en suite with bath and stunning ocean view. Don't be surprised to see seals playing in the waves below or whales migrating.

The entrance stairway that leads to sheer beauty and the light filled open plan first floor invites you to relax and take all before you in. The outside terrace and floor-to-ceiling ocean facing glass provides 180 degree views from Wye Point to Kennett River.

CASA ALTIPLANO

CASA ALTIPLANO

Jalisco, Mexico

Eccentric and glamorous are two words that come to mind when describing Costa Careyes, the unique community along the expansive coastline between Manzanillo and Puerto Vallarta in Mexico.

In 1968, Gian Franco Brignone, a famed banker and real estate developer from Turin, Italy spotted the then uninhabited stretch of sand and islands from a light aircraft. Without setting foot on shore, Brignone snapped up the almost 15 kilometers (approx. 9 miles) of coastline by wiring $2 million to a local friend's bank account. It would become the playground for aristocrats, billionaires, celebrities and playboys alike.

Costa Careyes is renowned for its 50 architecturally inspiring villas and Casa Altiplano, overlooking Playa Rosa, does not disappoint with its curious yet chic aesthetic.

The property is a combination of Mediterranean sensuality and clean, minimalist style. The infinity pool area includes a heated Jacuzzi, water feature, sundecks and outdoor shower.

Clinging dramatically to the cliff edge, Casa Altipano is an elegant mix of natural materials mixed with a modern take of adobe brick construction and an expansive central palapa – an open-sided dwelling with a thatched roof made of dried palm leaves. The main house, with its bold yellow and black stripe design, acts as a contrast to the older style, rustic elements.

The living room and dining areas are situated under the palapa while the main house boasts five bedrooms with en suites. The master bedroom is the perfect parent's retreat with its own living room and terrace with divine garden outlook.

The coastal landscape, complimented by an infinity pool, dreamy loungers atop generous sun decks, urge you to take in the magnificent view.

Costa Careyes maintains its bohemian roots which means homeowners not only need several million dollars to buy in, they must meet 27 conditions such as being multilingual, appreciating the music of sky, earth and sea, as well as having committed most of the seven deadly sins.

The yellow and black striped main house is bold and dramatic and acts as a counterpoint to the traditional and rustic elements.

The rustic, dining area seats twelve, the scene of many a memorable meal where you have the option of preparing it yourself in the gourmet kitchen or calling on the private chef to turn fresh, local fare into a gourmet feast.

Photos by Mark Callanan

LA CASA

LA CASA

Jumby Bay, West Indies

This exquisite British Colonial style villa – 930 square meters (10,000 square feet) – is set on 1.2 hectares (three acres) of lush tropical gardens. The home is located on the breathtaking coral sands of Pasture Bay.

Inside the house you'll find a drawing room, dining room and a modern, fully equipped kitchen. The library with vaulted wood ceiling and overstuffed sofas offers the perfect spot to curl up with a good book.

The master bedroom, on the second floor, features bespoke furnishings with an en suite bathroom complete with claw foot soaking tub. The suite opens onto a furnished private balcony that overlooks the pool and beach.

Overlooking the coral sands of Pasture Bay, covered terraces with graceful archways and beamed ceilings and sumptuous furnishings bring an indoor feel to the outdoors.

Adjacent to the pool is the private croquet lawn. The property also features a tennis court and gym for those who like to stay active.

From an upper level terrace, the pool draws the eye to the ocean.

Mere steps from the beach sits the property's inviting swimming pool and jacuzzi. The pool deck features generous sun lounges, flowing vines and tropical plants. Swim, relax under the umbrella or make use of the poolside bar.

Two additional bedrooms with en suite bathrooms make up the main house but if a crowd is coming to stay, La Casa also has three separate guest cottages.

Each of the five bedrooms has an en suite bathroom of grand proportions.

Footsteps from the beach are the property's swimming pool and jacuzzi. The spacious pool deck is filled with wrought iron lounges and gorgeous flowering plants and vines. Behind the pool are covered terraces with graceful archways and beamed ceilings.

LAZY LIZARD

LAZY LIZARD

West Indies

A luxurious fusion of Caribbean and Asian architecture defines this exceptional beachfront estate. The property is essentially a series of eight pavilions gathered around a spectacular free form swimming pool with floating dining pavilion – all set on two tropical hectares (5 acres).

Conceived as an escape for friends and family, the design is testament to the relaxed, serene and elegant ambience (and very social nature) of the property.

The six bedroom suites are housed in separate pavilions surrounding the main house which includes two master suites with amazing views of the sea.

The large free form swimming pool with tropical landscaped gardens is the focal point of the estate which fuses Caribbean and Asian architecture.

The free form swimming pool has a sunken lounge area the extends into the pool – the ideal spot to stay cool on hot days.

Each bedroom suite features large living areas with sleek and stylish en suite baths, custom stonework and private outdoor gardens with rain showers.

The two master bathrooms feature baths carved from ivory travertine (a form of limestone). The spacious open air living and dining room, contemporary kitchen, media room and office open onto a spectacular swimming pool set in the middle of the estate with a floating dining pavilion.

A short stroll away is the estate's tennis court with pavilion and fitness centre.

AVE HOUSE

AVE HOUSE

Lima, Peru

Architect, Martin Dulanto Sangalli, describes his stunning contemporary design as "a white box, a habitat platform. The space generated between both elements composes this project."

Located in Cerro Azul (Blue Hill) – a fishing village 131 kilometers (81 miles) south of Lima – this five-bedroom, six-bathroom home, built in 2014, is spread across three levels.

The basement has the living room, the fourth and fifth bedrooms with bathrooms and a terrace. The central staircase leads to the ground level featuring the courtyard, living room, kitchen, terrace with barbecue and sunbathing area, pool, guest bathroom and the service bedroom and bathroom.

Another level up reveals the master bedroom with balcony, master bathroom and the second and third bedrooms with bathrooms.

Martin Dulanto Sangalli further explains his design.

"The box is separated from the base creating a large space open to the landscape. The white block contains the master bedroom, which runs through the whole front of the house, facing the sea, and the two guest bedrooms, located on the back of the lot. These three rooms are organized around a hall, which reaches the staircase, and also connects all three levels.

"The 'space between' of the first level contains all social areas (hall, dining room and the terrace room) in a single large space, fully integrated. This is the level of access into the project. In addition, within this space is a box, painted purple, containing the entire service area, including the kitchen.

In the basement you can find the two remaining bedrooms of the family, along with the den. Such spaces are organized around the stair hall and are connected by the terrace facing the sea."

Waking up to the view framed by floor to ceiling glass, the master bedroom runs the whole length of the front of the house.

Photos by Juan Solano

OLEANDER

OLEANDER

Antigua, West Indies

Classical Caribbean architecture and colonial-style décor and furnishings blend beautifully in this elegant estate home on Pasture Bay.

Six generous bedrooms with en suite bathrooms are encased by two large verandahs at the front and back of the waterfront property.

A tranquil paradise in the midst of Antigua, Oleander's breathtaking sea views and 1.2 hectares (3 acres) of manicured gardens come together with the inviting swimming pool and pool house for perfect indoor/outdoor living.

Oleander's interiors are the perfect balance of chic beach living and estate elegance. With columned verandas at the front and back, louvered doors and white vaulted ceilings, Oleander's living room is a nod to traditional Caribbean architecture.

The white Hamptons style kitchen is fully equipped to whip up a gourmet meal or have your private chef rattle the pans.

One of the six bedrooms at Oleanader, this one blends the chic beach feel with more traditional influences – dark wood four poster bed, white French doors and white bedding with turquoise accents.

ST IVES

ST IVES

Cornwell, England

Interior designer, Suzy Fairfield, was lured by one of the oldest homes in St Ives, Cornwall to transform the charming but formerly claustrophobic and austere building that dates back to 1540, into an enchanting, light-filled six-bedroom home.

The ancient building's history has been respected, combining original features like the striking granite walls with contemporary additions. The home, tucked away in a quaint hillside street in the heart of St Ives, enjoys views over the town rooftops and out to see.

The third-floor master bedroom views out to sea do not disappoint whilst the spacious open-plan kitchen and dining area, featuring bi-fold doors that look out to the contemporary garden, is a fabulous space and heart of the home.

The property's seaside location influenced the crisp, clean palette of cool, neutral colors with understated touches such as ticking linen and bleached nautical stripes, carefully sourced to set the perfect tone for laidback coastal living.

Photos by Andreas von Einsiedel

ELIA VILLA

ELIA VILLA

Mykonos, Greece

The dreamy Cycladic architecture combination of white and blue is perfectly presented in this contemporary take on the traditional at Elia Villa. Water is visible from every corner of the property, either Elia, Agrari beaches or the vast infinity pool will be in your sight.

Overlooking Elia Beach on the Greek island of Mykonos, Elia Villa was designed with three elements in mind – white, stone and water. The whitewashed exterior and interior is mostly neutral and simple with splashes of color in the form of art, antique pieces and furnishings.

The smooth curved edges of the villa spread over four levels. The upper level is home to the living space, kitchen and a bathroom. One floor above this is a dreamy bedroom and bathroom with such breathtaking water views you'll think you're floating out to sea on a boat. Another master bedroom and bathroom on the ground floor has equally stunning views and below that, on the lower level is a second living space with three bedrooms and bathrooms.

The six cave-like bathrooms of the villa are made of polished concrete and appear to be carved out of the walls.

A dip in the infinity pool will have you thinking you could dive straight into the azure blue sea from there.

Sunset with its symphony of colors in the sky and on the sea is the perfect time to relax with a cocktail under the shade of the pergola. The Cliffside white Cycladic five bedroom villa enjoys uninterrupted ocean views and direct access to the Elia beach.

DEZANOVE HOUSE

DEZANOVE HOUSE

Galicia, Spain

Dezanove House, an award-winning home with splendid sea views, is situated on an almost private beach in a small fishing village in the Arousa estuary in Spain's northwest.

Designed by Spanish architect Inaki Leite, the three-bedroom, four-bathroom home was inspired by the natural coastal environment. It incorporates charmingly weathered recycled 'bateas' wood – the platforms placed at sea by the local mussel fisherman along the natural rock faces.

The wood is exposed to everything the sea and coastal weather can throw at it for over 25 years before being sent to recycling, usually for use in vineyards or gardens.

Inaki Leite's use of this wood in architecture is innovative. The beams were treated and halved to yield two diverse surfaces. The outer of the wood beam kept the original rough texture and was used for the outer façade whilst the inside cut of the beam was used within the interior to provide visual warmth which has a Scandinavian-inspired aesthetic.

The design also incorporates the naked rock that protects the home and also opens up the space to the sea and sunlight..

The main floor features a sizeable south facing glass wall showcasing sea and garden views with a fireplace and lounge area and an oak-panelled kitchen, perfect for entertaining family and friends.

The exposed concrete and stainless steel staircase takes you to the master bedroom with en suite, and a rooftop terrace with retractable shutters, as well as an extra terrace bedroom with separate bath. Another stairway leads to the main entrance and two bedrooms on the ground floor.

As well as the use of locally sourced materials, every section of the home was created by local craftsmen, including the finishes and furnishings.

The energy efficient home with solar power, insulation and ventilation systems and a purifying vertical moss garden was thoughtfully designed with respect to nature and the environment.

The house borrows from the tradition of the surroundings and reveals itself through its design and detailing. Protected by rock and open to the sea views, the living room faces south to capture the warmth of the sun.

The age of the wood is not hidden. The different outer and inner faces of the wood are used to create different sensations. In the living room, the wood is purposely set to frame and direct the view to the exterior.

Contemporary and minimalist, the bathrooms – like the rest of the home – are environmentally friendly and energy efficient, bringing in great natural light.

The building process was challenging with the shape and slope of the plot, the local planning restrictions and the very hard rock found on the back of the site.

The space is divided into two interconnecting levels. The more private one can be closed from the outside and protected from the sun with the folding wooden shutters facing south. The house resembles the old booths on top of the mussel platforms, and similarly to them, some parts of the house seem to float.

Photos by Adrian Vasquez

AZURIS

AZURIS

Hamilton Island, Australia

Idyllically located on the western side of Hamilton Island, the aptly named Azuris overlooking the Coral Sea, is one of two holiday homes nestled side-by-side that architect Renato D'Ettorre designed for the same client.

The three bedroom design spectacularly responds to three key elements of its location – light, air and water.

Indoor and outdoor effortlessly blend and spaces fuse, making the most of ocean breezes and light. The sea is not just the focus of the view but also wraps around the main pavilion in the form of a spacious infinity pool, blending seamlessly into the horizon and the ocean vista.

Airflow is optimized and adjusted with walls and shading devices easily opened, creating comfort, reducing the need for airconditioning and artificial lighting.

Although stunning, the design brief included instruction for a low-maintenance house that is all about easy living.

Situated on a site that falls steeply away to the water's edge, on approach, the only part of the house visible is a green roof planted with native species, which further draw the eye out towards the horizon and the spectacular view.

The contemporary design adopts a pavilion form, with floor to ceiling sliding glass doors, bedrooms and living areas spread over three levels. Internal courtyards are tranquil spaces of pools and ponds.

Construction materials are concrete, stone and glass – chosen for their rawness and transparency respectively. The house spans between two dominant walls. The living area, main bedroom and pool are on the top level for privacy, with guest rooms and an undercover sheltered terrace on the lower level. The western façade opens up entirely to the view whilst the two side walls and natural stone wall anchor the home into the earth.

The site, abundant with wildlife and covered in eucalypts and a mangrove swamp, needed to respect the flora and fauna. With water scarce on the island, 40,000 liters (8,800 gallons) of rainwater is collected in tanks within the basement. Water is also recycled, treated and used to water the landscape.

The open upper living area embraces an outdoor/indoor lifestyle. Azuris' design responds to three key elements of its island location – light, air and water.

The entry courtyard is shielded from the road by high stone walls. The courtyard is a quiet contemplative place with a cooling reflection pond with waterlilies. The entrance courtyard opens directly onto the main living floor. A steel barbecue has been integrated into the massive stone wall, creating a casual outdoor cooking zone not far from the kitchen and dining area.

The house sits inconspicuously into the landscape so that is difficult to imagine what lies beyond the unobtrusive external walls.

Photos by Francesco Giovanelli

SEGEDIN HOUSE

SEGEDIN HOUSE

Mt Maunganui, New Zealand

This comfortable yet elegant four bedroom beach house in Mt Maunganui, a town in the Bay of Plenty of New Zealand's North Island, was designed to connect the stunning outdoors with a simple, refined interior.

Designed by Eva Nash of Rogan Nash Architects in Auckland, the house is a collection of spaces, which allow the light to pour in whilst centering around the living areas and the generously proportioned fireplace.

Inviting yet sophisticated, this house works equally well as a family holiday retreat and a permanent residence.

The coastal location was inspiration for the house, conceived as two distinct pavilions separated by a glass walkway and a large sheltered courtyard. The front pavilion has over-sized glass sliding doors and allows for all the living and entertaining spaces. The rear pavilion is built of concrete block and contains four bedrooms and three and a half bathrooms. The courtyard design maximizes the sun and views while providing shelter from the coastal winds.

The house is oriented to make the most of the sun, to create warm light-filled living areas, minimizing the need for artificial lighting and heating. Louvres on the northern façade of the house allow for shading to the large areas of glass which avoids overheating.

Concrete block (both exposed and rendered) was used in the construction of the home as well as glass and steel.

The front pavilion is seaward-facing and uses large glass doors and exposed structural steel to create alight-filled open plan living area. Honed concrete block is used internally to act as a heat sink, as well as a visual anchor for the fireplace.

The rear pavilion is private and solid built from concrete block which continues from exterior to interior.

The house, built for Eva Nash's mother in 2005, and modified in 2013, is a favorite project of the architect. "I particularly like the exposed structural steel in the living room," says Eva. "The honesty of this material gives an aesthetic lightness to the space while providing visual interest."

ALINGHI BEACH HOUSE

ALINGHI BEACH HOUSE

Agnes Water, Queensland, Australia

With the basic philosophy of having as little impact as possible on the environment, Alinghi, was designed by award-winning Australian architect, James Grose of Bligh Voller Nield (BVN) and voted one of the world's top five beach houses.

The house is one of six homes situated in the exclusive Rocky Point estate, consisting of 5.5 hectares (14 acres) of bushland and sitting on absolute beachfront, approximately six kilometers (3.5 miles) south of Agnes Water in Queensland.

Renowned for environmentally sensitive design, James Grose's idea was to create a sanctuary which allowed the home owner to live a tranquil lifestyle amongst nature without foregoing style and luxury.

Upon arrival, walking down the stairs to what seems like thick bushland, the sounds of the ocean envelop you, then, at the last step, amazing views of the Pacific Ocean open before you.

Alinghi has been described as a 'floating shipping container' – albeit a luxurious one – built to feel like you're floating on the ocean.

Two pavilions form the accommodation linked by a concrete-covered way. The main pavilion is designed with large living spaces opening onto a variety of semi-enclosed areas providing retreat from the wind or for basking in the Queensland sun.

The second pavilion is a retreat with bedroom and private study. Both buildings are adjacent to the travertine platform on the north and south and to the west, the open concrete walkway framing the bush (travertine is a form of limestone).

The main pavilion and retreat pavilion are situated around a central stone terrace overhanging the ocean. With a view to die for and the gentle sound of waves crashing below, doors off the bedrooms open completely to make the most of the sights and the sounds.

External materials and colors were wisely chosen to 'disappear' over time, fading to a silver grey, blending with the landscape and the silvery bark of the trees. Arctic cedar clads the exterior of the house. Hardy and low maintenance, the timber has faded beautifully with exposure to the Queensland sun.

Alinghi is self-sufficient for water with tanks collecting abundant rainfall, whilst airconditioning is unnecessary as clever design, allowing cross-ventilation, and the position of the house combine to allow cool ocean breezes to waft throughout. As the sun rises and sets, different areas of Alinghi allow shelter from the sun at different times of the day.

Alinghi, along with the five other houses on the estate, share a private beach at Honeymoon Bay, a 30 meter (32 yard) saltwater swimming pool by the ocean, entertaining cabana with barbecue facilities and grass tennis court.

Wildlife such as wallabies, echidnas, goannas, turtles and a diversity of birds are plentiful. Purposely designed, Alinghi's external lighting is all low-voltage so as not to upset the neighbourly creatures, in particular nesting turtles whom return to Rocky Point to breed.

Despite being the ultimate in luxury, the residence is architecturally designed to be environmentally sensitive. The eco-friendly beachfront hideaway boasts sleek interiors and state of the art technology.

Photos by John Gollings

LINK HOUSE

LINK HOUSE

Sydney, Australia

Located on the Sydney Harbour foreshore in Chiswick, the home's owner built his vision on the original site of his childhood home.

The design brief for Renato D'Ettorre Architects was to separate the living and sleeping quarters for this busy, young family who love to entertain.

Completed in 2012, the design attempts to blur the edges between indoors and outdoors whilst maintaining privacy as well as openness and maximizing the spectacular water views across Five Dock Bay.

The public space of the living area is housed in a glass pavilion with large glass folding doors which can be opened to bring the outside in. The pavilion, surrounded by gardens, terraces and breezeways, emphasizes the bay environment, the sun, the breezes and the views.

The pavilion space also houses the kitchen, dining and sitting areas, fireplace, and a rooftop terrace to showcase the spectacular water views.

The sleeping quarters pavilion is over three levels. The children's bedrooms and bathrooms are on the entry level, a lounge area, utility spaces, commercial kitchen and steam room occupy the second and third levels with the parent's master bedroom on the top level which also includes a rooftop courtyard, vegetable garden and orchard.

The owners had seen one of architect Renato D'Ettore's earlier concrete houses and wanted a similar construction utilizing low-maintenance materials.

The two pavilions are joined at ground level by a glass link spanning a large fish pond, surrounded by an internal garden and courtyard. Featuring a fixed glass floor and roof, its retractable glass walls open to the south-facing courtyard and north-facing garden.

The internal courtyard is the heart of the family home. It's the perfect space for gathering family and friends for a barbecue or pizza from the home's pizza oven.

The owner, a passionate foodie who works within the food industry, wanted a concrete bench in the kitchen, a walk-in fridge and separate domestic and industrial kitchens.

The architect says: "We've created a robust house with durability without making it look industrial."

"The roof terrace is my favorite space," says architect, Renato D'Ettorre. "It is where the sun can be enjoyed throughout most of the day in summer and winter. It beckons the visitor upon entering the house to explore the terrace and the panoramic view of the surrounding bay and gardens."

Photos by Murray Fredericks

SEASCAPE

SEASCAPE

Pigeon Bay, Canterbury, New Zealand

The ultimate romantic escape, Seascape Retreat is a stunning beachside cottage, conceived and designed by Auckland architect, Andrew Patterson of Patterson Associates.

Accessible only by helicopter or 4-wheel-drive vehicle, this award-winning home is set into a rock escarpment in a tiny boulder strewn South Pacific cove on New Zealand's South Island.

With the snowcapped Southern Alps to the west and the Pacific Ocean on your doorstep, the Canterbury region is approximately an hour south of Christchurch. The retreat consists of just three rooms – a lobby, living/sleeping area and bathroom. The open plan includes a main living area, with split-level separation between the bedroom area, with glass walls overlooking the ocean.

A modern, sleek kitchen is off to the side whilst the cave-like bathroom at the back, with its deep freestanding tub with view out to the terrace, also takes in the breathtaking view of this area known for its vast territory of grassy surrounds, sparkling lakes and snow-capped mountains.

Constructed using local materials, largely using rock quarried nearby, steel, glass, in-situ poured concrete floors and an earth turfed roof, the structure is seamlessly integrated into the escarpment above to protect occupants from falling debris.

The cottage is self-sustainable – it has on-site water harvesting and a wastewater treatment system.

The overall plan is an interlocking geometry responding to both near views of the bay and far views out to rocky spires. The house is lined with horizontal macrocarpa wood (macrocarpa is a Californian cypress tree with a large spreading crown of horizontal branches and leaves that smell of lemon when crushed).

This timber forms integrated joinery, wall and ceiling panels behind double glazed low e-glass in storm and shatter proof steel mullions which utilize earthquake resistant sliding heads. Such features are essential given Christchurch (also on New Zealand's southern island) has been struck by two large earthquakes in recent times.

The dramatic rock, concrete and sleek design is softened with soft neutral textiles, animal hides and contemporary furnishings that include the suspended Eero Aarnio Bubble chair – the perfect spot for reading, taking in the view or relaxing in front of the fire with a glass of wine. The outdoor lounge area with fireplace and spa pool complete the romantic dream. Simply add Champagne.

The interlocking geometric design corresponds to both views of the bay and distant views out to Rocky Spire appearing as if you are floating on the open sea.

The remote, secluded location along the Banks Peninsula of New Zealand's South Island in only accessible for helicopter or four-wheel drive.

FRESHWATER HOUSE

FRESHWATER HOUSE

Sydney, Australia

Perched high on the cliff above Freshwater on Sydney's northern beaches, Freshwater House is a harmonious design with the seaside landscape that celebrates its spectacular location with contemporary architecture uniquely crafted for a young family. It's functional, versatile and filled with light and endless views.

The masterfully engineered three split-level construction spans 520 square meters (622 square yards) and yet remains home-like and comfortable whilst optimizing all that is Freshwater.

Standing within the house, you literally feel you're within the landscape. Set into the escarpment, the design utilizes its layers to create space delineation and zoning across the split-levels. The sun, breeze and light have all influenced the project.

The home features five bedrooms, three en suites, two bathrooms with separate WC, children's playroom, lounge, dining and substantial kitchen. Then there's the cocktail bar, games room, three-car garage, pool, spa, sauna, theatre room, gymnasium, study and 17 square meter (20 square yards) walk-in master wardrobe.

The indoor spaces all lead seamlessly outdoors, taking advantage of the two-hundred-degree ocean views.

Architect Poune Parsanejad: "Every design decision, angle and framing utilizes the magic surrounding the house. The views, light, breezes and framing out of neighbours properties, all command focus upon the sand, waves, sun rise and set and evening light display."

Photos by Brett Boardman

AMANZI KAMALA

AMANZI KAMAL

Cape Sol Villa, Phuket, Thailand

Nestled in a cascading, west facing ravine in a secluded spot along Cape Amarin on the west coast of Phuket is Amanzi Kamal. With stunning views over the azure blue Andaman Sea, it's easy to see why the exclusive area, where Amanzi Kamala sits, is known as Millionaire's Mile.

Set in a densely forested cliff above the water's edge, Original Vision architects' principal defining element is the rock.

The architect's commission to do this demanding but ultimately spectacular site justice was both daunting and exciting.

The focal point of this ultra modern 2,644 square meter (3,162 square yard) design, laid out over three traversing levels, is the cantilevered glass bottomed swimming pool, drawing the eye to the stunning view.

The main floor comprises spacious open plan living areas, with the granite rock face defining one edge, and large folding glass panelled walls that open the entire floor into an open-air pavilion overlooking the pool and ocean. The entire home appears to grow out from the rock and extends through the living areas, the upper terraces and down the steep jungle path to the secluded shale beach below.

Above the main floor is the main bedroom which is level with the master suite and three other bedrooms all with bathrooms, each with impressive, continuous ocean views. Sliding doors can be opened to allow ocean breezes to cool the spaces.

Below the main floor are two more bedrooms with bathrooms, a large games and family room and private spa. Access to steps leading to rock pools and the ocean below is from this level.

The property is dramatically proportioned overall, adapting to its environment with outdoors and indoors becoming one integrated space. The living spaces are enhanced by the lush, tropical private gardens that have been planted over two levels.

A simple but dramatic version of luxury and sharp architectural design highlights the beauty of the surrounds.

OUTDOOR BEACH STYLE

OUTDOOR STYLE LIVING

Outdoor style and design on the coast needs to be designed understanding the exposures living near the water, particularly gardens need to feature robust plants that are able to cope with salt exposure, high winds and soils that can hold water and nutrients.

Subtropical plants like ferns, palms, *Echium vulgare*, *Erigeron glaucus* 'Sea Breeze', *Rosmarinus officinalis*, Bromeliads, Sea Kale to name a few.

Some gardeners prefer to feature plants in pots as many plants can not survive or grow in sandy conditions and with good soil and a shady environment plants can survive as long as they are hardy plants that can flourish in hot environments.

Creating a unique outdoor space using rocks, concrete steps or features, outdoor lounge or dining furniture, clay or strong cement pots, curtains and cushions, wood panels or features, day beds, or anything that carries the design style from inside to out.

Many landscape designers believe simple and hardy plants featuring stunning pot designs with good soil and water access can benefit any garden and style you are after in your coastal garden.

Style your garden with hedges for privacy, hardy pots weighed down for windy conditions, bright cushions on outdoor furniture, and anything that suits your lifestyle whether it be your primary residence or you holiday home.

Photos: Shutterstock

ACKNOWLEDGEMENTS

A special thanks to the individuals, photographers and companies who gave their time during the production of this book. It is possible to 'live the dream' with some of these beach houses. The residences below can be leased through the following.

Alinghi, Agnes Water, Queensland, Australia
www.alinghi.com.au

Boutique Homes
www.boutique-homes.com
Casa Altiplano, Jalisco, Mexico
Tulum Villa, Yucatan, Mexico
Casa Kalika, Punta Mita, Mexico
Dezanove House, Galicia, Spain
Elia Villa, Mykonos, Greece
The White House, Santa Teresa, Costa Rica
Seascape Retreat, Pigeon Bay, Canterbury, New Zealand
Amanzi Kamala, Cape Sol, Phuket

Casa Kimball, Dominican Republic
www.casakimball.com

Rosewood Hotels
www.rosewoodhotels.com/en/jumby-bay-antigua
Frangipani, Jumby Bay, West Indies
La Casa, Jumby Bay, West Indies
Lazy Lizard, Jumby Bay, West Indies
Oleander, Jumby Bay, West Indies

Sea Ranch, Mornington Peninsula, Victoria, Australia
www.searanch.com.au

Villa Azul Celeste, Puerto Vallarta, Mexico
www.villaazulceleste.net

First published in 2016 by New Holland Publishers
This edition published in 2022 by New Holland Publishers
Sydney

Level 1, 178 Fox Valley Road, Wahroonga, NSW 2076, Australia

newhollandpublishers.com

A record of this book is held at the National Library of Australia.

ISBN 9781760795450

Managing Director: Fiona Schultz
Editor: Susie Stevens
Design: Andrew Davies
Production Director: Arlene Gippert
Printed in China

10 9 8 7 6 5 4 3 2 1

Keep up with New Holland Publishers:
NewHollandPublishers
@newhollandpublishers

US $24.99